"Super-Hungry Mice Eat Onions"

and Other Painless Tricks for Memorizing Geography Facts

BRIAN P. CLEARY

Illustrated by J. P. SANDY

M Millbrook Press · Minneapolis

To my daughter Ellen
—B.P.C.

To Joyce, Eric, and Michael
—J.P.S.

Millbrook Press
A division of Lerner Publishing Group, Inc.
241 First Avenue North
Minneapolis, MN 55401 U.S.A.

Website address: www.lernerbooks.com

Library of Congress Cataloging-in-Publication Data

Cleary, Brian P., 1959-
    "Super-hungry mice eat onions" and other painless tricks for memorizing geography facts / by Brian P. Cleary ; illustrated by J. P. Sandy.
        p.   cm. – (Adventures in memory)
    Includes index.
    ISBN: 978-0-8225-7820-8 (lib. bdg. : alk. paper)
    1. Geography—Miscellanea. 2. Mnemonics. I. Sandy, J. P., ill. II. Title.
G131.C64 2010
910–dc22   2008049644

Manufactured in the United States of America
1 2 3 4 5 6 - DP - 15 14 13 12 11 10

HOW THIS BOOK WILL HELP YOU MEMORIZE GEOGRAPHY FACTS

Mnemonic
(pronounced *nih-MAH-nik*)

is a fancy word given to little tricks or devices that help us memorize important facts. Some of them rhyme, such as,

"Columbus sailed the ocean blue in fourteen hundred ninety-two."

Other memory aids build a word made up of the first letters of a list we're trying to memorize. **ROY G. BIV** is a trick for remembering the colors of the rainbow in order (**R**ed, **O**range, **Y**ellow, **G**reen, **B**lue, **I**ndigo, and **V**iolet). The made-up name ROY G. BIV contains the first letter of the name of each color.

Still other memory tools are more visual, meaning that a picture will help us to remember a fact, such as this one: A **Bactrian** camel has a back shaped like the letter **"B"** turned on its side. A **Dromedary** camel has a back shaped like the letter **"D"** turned on its side. So we know a Bactrian camel has two humps and a Dromedary camel has one.

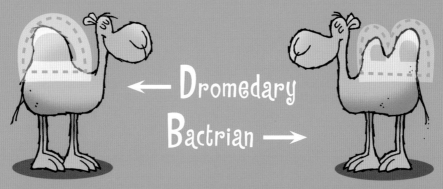

← Dromedary

Bactrian →

In this book, you'll find lots of fun ways to memorize geography facts. But what I'm really hoping is that you'll develop your own tricks. Oftentimes the words, silly rhymes, or crazy sentences that you invent will be the most meaningful way for you to master geography!

Here's an example of what I thought of to memorize the five great lakes in order of size: **SUPER-HU**ngry **MIC**e **E**at **ON**ions. That stands for: **SUPER**ior, **HU**ron, **MIC**higan, **E**rie, and **ON**tario. But let's say you have a friend named Emily who is always doing funny things. It might be more meaningful (and therefore memorable) for you to say:

Seven **H**amburgers **M**ade **E**mily **O**verfed.

Sometimes, it's the absurd nature of what you've come up with that will help you to remember. They say that elephants never forget. Well, now that you know about mnemonics, neither will you!

UP, DOWN, AND ALL AROUND

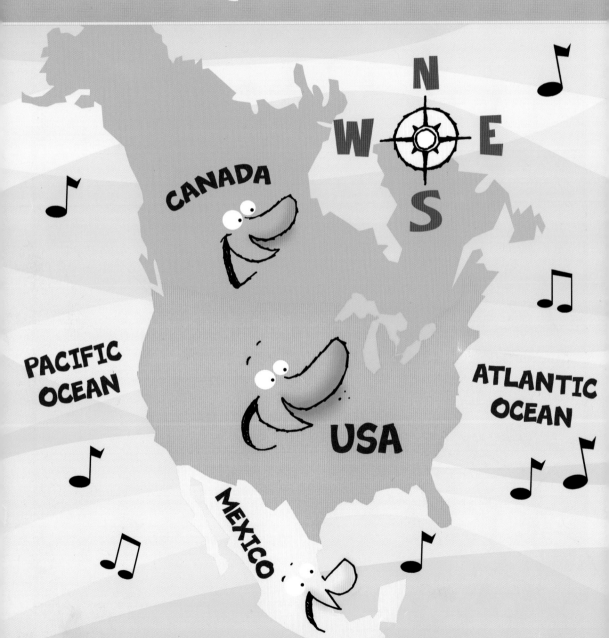

As we look at a map of North America, north is at the top, south is at the bottom, west is to the left, and east is to the right. So get out your maps and SING! Sing this song to the tune of "If You're Happy and You Know It."

Just above the USA is Can-a-da.
Just above the USA is Can-a-da.
Just above it, not below it,
on a map, it's sure to show it.
Just above the USA is Can-a-da.

↓

Just below the USA is Mex-i-co.
Just below the USA is Mex-i-co.
Not above it but below it,
every map is sure to show it.
Just below the USA is Mex-i-co.

The Pacific is the ocean on the left.
The Pacific is the ocean on the left.
Way out west by California—
if you're tested, I should warn ya—
the Pacific is the ocean on the left.

↓

The Atlantic is the ocean on the right
The Atlantic is the ocean on the right.
You can sing it, you can shout it,
but there is no need to doubt it.
The Atlantic is the ocean on the right.

READ ON!
How much do you know about our neighbors to the north and south? Read *Canada* by Janice Hamilton and *Mexico* by Tom Streissguth to learn more.

AT 13 COLONY STREET

The original thirteen colonies (by line in the poem) are:

CONnecticut, **NEW HAM**pshire / **VIRGINIA**, **MARY**land / **DELa**Ware /
NEW JERSEY / **MAS**sachusetts / South Carolina / Pennsylvania /
GEORGIA, Rhode Island / **NEW YORK** / North CArolina.

CONrad got a **NEW HAM**ster,
he named **VIRGINIA MARY**.
He asked his cousin **DEL**la Where
she found one, fat and hairy.

They dressed it in a **NEW JERSEY**
and brought it to her **MA'S**.
The **S**hirt **C**ompletely covered it
except for head and **P**aws.

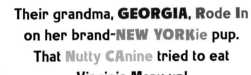

Their grandma, **GEORGIA**, Rode In
on her brand-**NEW YORK**ie pup.
That Nutty CAnine tried to eat
Virginia Mary up!

EXTRA CREDIT

On July 4, 1776, the thirteen colonies declared
independence from Great Britain. The colonies became the
first thirteen states in the United States of America.

THESE LAKES ARE GREAT!

The five Great Lakes, in order of size, are **SUPERior**, **HUron**, **MIChigan**, **Erie**, **and ONtario**. These lakes are listed from biggest to smallest area. Area is the amount of space the surface of the lake takes up. That's not the same as how much water each lake holds. That measurement is volume.

SUPER-Hungry MICe Eat ONions

EXTRA CREDIT

The word *superior* means "the best"—and best takes first place! So remember that Lake Superior is number one when it comes to size. "Ontario" begins and ends with what looks like a zero. Zero is the smallest number. And Lake Ontario is the smallest of the Great Lakes.

NiFTY, NiFTY, THEY MADE 50!

If you're ever asked on a test to name in order the last two states to join the United States, you should relax, take a deep breath, and say:

The **A** and the **H** stand for Alaska and Hawaii. Alaska is number forty-nine, and Hawaii is fifty. They both joined the United States in the year 1959.

GOING TO TOWN

A Song about the Ten Largest U.S. Cities (in terms of population)

In order, the ten U.S. cities with the highest populations (as of 2009) are:

1. New York City, New York
2. Los Angeles, California
3. Chicago, Illinois
4. Houston, Texas
5. Philadelphia, Pennsylvania
6. Phoenix, Arizona
7. San Antonio, Texas
8. San Diego, California
9. Dallas, Texas
10. San Jose, California

READ ON!

Learn about the biggest U.S. cities and much more in *United States in Pictures* by Tom Streissguth.

Number one is NEW YORK CITY.
In the eastern region there,
you will spot 'er, near the water,
giant buildings everywhere.

Number two is named LOS AN-GE-LES,
and it's sometimes called L.A.
It's out west, where folks are blest
with sunny skies most every day.

Third's CHICAGO, fourth is HOUSTON.
PHIL-A-DEL-PH-IA is five,
where a nation took formation,
so it could be free and thrive.

Sixth is PHOENIX, ARIZONA.
Seven's SAN ANTONIO.
Eight's a city, warm and pretty,
SAN-DI-E-GO, don't you know!

Ninth is DALLAS—it's in Texas,
where so much is big, and then
next in line, right after nine,
it's SAN JOSE at number ten.

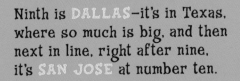

FIVE IN ONE

The United States has five regions. Think of the fifty states or the fifty stars on the U.S. flag, and use the five from that number to remind you of the country's five regions. The regions are **NORtheast**, **Midwest**, **SouthEast**, **WEst**, and **SouthWEst**. Read more about each region on the following pages.

NORTHEAST
Maine, New Hampshire, Vermont, New York, Pennsylvania, New Jersey, Connecticut, Massachusetts, Rhode Island, Delaware, Maryland

WEST
Washington, Oregon, Idaho, Montana, Wyoming, Colorado, Utah, Nevada, California, Hawaii, Alaska

MIDWEST
North Dakota, South Dakota, Minnesota, Wisconsin, Michigan, Kansas, Ohio, Illinois, Iowa, Missouri, Nebraska, Indiana

SOUTHWEST
Arizona, New Mexico, Texas, Oklahoma

SOUTHEAST
Virginia, West Virginia, Kentucky, Tennessee, North Carolina, South Carolina, Georgia, Florida, Alabama, Mississippi, Arkansas, Louisiana

When you need to remember what the regions are, think of this phrase:

NORma Made SEveral

WEird SWEaters

WEST

Let's use this jump rope song to memorize the western states.

I'm going out west—
gonna wear
my red bandanna—
WASHINGTON,
OREGON,
IDAHO, MONTANA!

I'm going out west,
gonna do
a little roaming—
UTAH,
CALIFORNIA,
NEVADA, and
WYOMING!

I'm going out west,
on a plane
or boat or auto—
ALASKA,
HAWAII,
even COLORADO!

EXTRA CREDIT

The westernmost town in the United States is Adak, Alaska.

SOUTHWEST

You can easily remember the four states of the Southwest region when you remember the phrase "a ton."

Arizona

Texas
Oklahoma
New Mexico

NORTHEAST

How will you remember this song for this region? The Northeast is the first place in the United States where the sun rises each day! (Sing this song to the tune of "You Are My Sunshine.")

Out in the Northeast,
the chilly Northeast,
you'll find eleven states are there—
Maine, Mass-a-chusetts, New York,
New Jersey, Connect-i-cut, and Del-a-ware.
You'll see New Hampshire
and Pennsylvania, Rhode Island,
Mary-land, Vermont.
I know eleven
(not six or seven).
I can re-peat them
if you want!

One more time!

MIDWEST

Get out your jump ropes again! This time we're memorizing the twelve states that make up the Midwest!

My mom and your mom
drove without rest
through all twelve states
of the great Midwest.

Mich-i-gan, Ohio,
Kansas, North Da-ko-ta,
Nebraska, Indiana,
Missouri, Minn-e-sota,

Illinois and Iowa,
Wisconsin, South Dakota—
where they fin-a-lly stopped
for a burger and a soda!

M-I-D-W-E-S-T!

BURGER

SOUTHEAST

Sing this to the tune of the ABC song or "Baa, Baa, Black Sheep" or "Twinkle, Twinkle, Little Star." Ever notice all three songs sound basically the same but with different words? Well, now there's a fourth one!

Virginia, Florida, Ten-nes-see,
both Carolinas, Miss-is-sip-pi,
West Virginia, Lou-i-si-an-a,
Ken-tuck-y and Al-a-bam-a,
Ar-kan-sas, and Georgia too—
I know the Southeast,
how about you?

MIXED-UP COUNTRY

Rearrange the letters in each cartoon caption to answer these geographical riddles. Find the answers on page 46.

This is the tallest mountain in the United States. It is in Alaska and is sometimes called Denali. It is 20,320 feet (6,194 meters) tall.

(Hint: The answer is two words.)

Yuck, lemon mint!

This California location is the lowest point in the United States. It is 282 feet (86 m) below sea level.

(Hint: The answer is two words.)

Tall, heavy Ed

This California mountain is the tallest mountain in the contiguous United States. It is 14,505 feet (4,421 m) tall.

(Hint: The answer is two words.)

Tiny women hut

EXTRA CREDIT

Contiguous means "next to." The contiguous United States includes all the states except Alaska and Hawaii. The highest point in the contiguous United States is only 85 miles (137 kilometers) from the lowest point in the United States.

At 2,466 miles (3,969 km) long, it's the longest river in the United States.

(Hint: The answer is three words. The first word is *the*.)

Sir, our rim thieves!

Officially, this is the first state in the United States. On December 7, 1787, it became the first of the original thirteen colonies to ratify (approve) the U.S. Constitution.

Weld area

EXTRA CREDIT

The state insect of this state is the ladybug.

Just 1,545 square miles (4,002 sq. km) in size, it's the smallest state in the United States.

(Hint: The answer is two words.)

Rhino saddle

It's the capital of the United States.

Watchdogs Inn

EXTRA CREDIT

From 1790 to 1800, Philadelphia, Pennsylvania, was the capital of the United States.

A MILLION TO ONE

Back in 2006, the population of the United States reached 300 million people. That year Wexler Middle School had exactly 304 students. Fifth grader Skippy Corrigan came up with a neat project that involved the giant map painted in the school's parking lot. He realized that if 300 students stood on the map, every student could represent 1 million people. Skippy still had 4 extra students. He gave them each a giant letter to tape to their heads. The letters N, E, W, and S stand for North, East, West, and South.

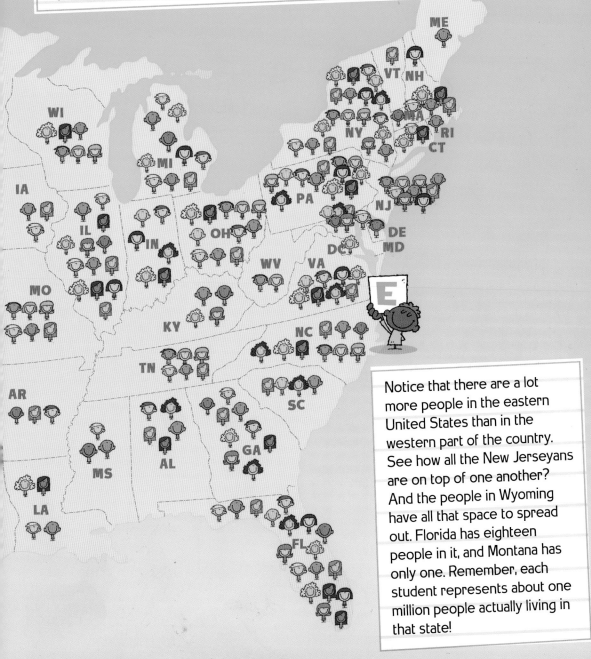

Notice that there are a lot more people in the eastern United States than in the western part of the country. See how all the New Jerseyans are on top of one another? And the people in Wyoming have all that space to spread out. Florida has eighteen people in it, and Montana has only one. Remember, each student represents about one million people actually living in that state!

WATER, WATER EVERYWHERE

The world has five oceans. In order of size, they are **PAcific**, **ATlantic**, **Indian**, **SOuthern**, and **ARcTIC**.

PA's ATtire Is somewhat ARtistic

VERY CONTINENTAL

The seven continents in order from biggest to smallest are:

ASia, **AFrica**, **North America**, **South America**, **ANtarctica**, **Europe**, and **AUstralia**.

On the following pages, you'll find some fun facts about each continent.

ASHley's AFfectionate NAnny SAw ANdy Eat AUtos

A RHYME ABOUT ASIA

You'll find mountains and plateaus,
islands, archipelagoes,
the Caspian and Dead Sea too,
rice, and lots of strong bamboo.

A MATTER OF FACT

Asia is the largest continent.

Its biggest countries are
Russia, China, and India.

One amazing feature: The world's
third-longest river is in Asia.
It's the Yangtze River, and it is
3,915 miles (6,300 km) long.

EXTRA CREDIT

Russia is part of two continents. Most
of it is in Asia, but the western part
of the country is in Europe.

A RHYME ABOUT AFRICA

Split by the equator,
it has diamonds, gas, and gold,
deserts, many languages,
and fossils that are old.

A MATTER OF FACT

Africa is the second-largest continent.

Its biggest countries are Sudan, Algeria, and Democratic Republic of Congo.

One amazing feature: The tallest mountain in Africa is Mount Kilimanjaro. It is 19,340 feet (5,895 m) high.

AMHARIC
SWAHILI
WOLOF
AFRIKAANS
HAUSA
SHONA

EXTRA CREDIT

Have you heard of Anansi? Read about this West African trickster in the folktale *Anansi and the Box of Stories*, adapted by Stephen Krensky.

A RHYME ABOUT NORTH AMERICA

It's the grocer to the world,
growing corn
and wheat and grains,
with mountains high
and rivers long,
and broad, unbroken plains.

A MATTER OF FACT

North America is the
third-largest continent.

Its biggest countries are
Canada, the United States,
and Mexico.

One amazing feature: The
most populous city in North
America is Mexico City,
the capital of Mexico.
It has more than
8.8 million residents!

A RHYME ABOUT SOUTH AMERICA

Most speak Spanish, Portuguese,
English, French, or Dutch.
The land, that's mostly tropical,
produces fruit and such.

A MATTER OF FACT

South America is the
fourth-largest continent.

Its biggest countries are Brazil,
Argentina, and Peru.

One amazing feature: The world's
tallest waterfall, Angel Falls, is
in Venezuela. The waterfall's
height is 3,212 feet (979 m).

A RHYME ABOUT ANTARCTICA

Though millions of
miles in landmass,
Antarctica's still home
to no man.
If you'd like to live in
a climate like that,
you'd best be a penguin
or snowman.

A MATTER OF FACT

Antarctica is the fifth-largest
continent.

It has no countries.

One amazing feature: Antarctica
is covered by a huge sheet of ice.
This continent is not home to any
man, woman, boy, or girl. In fact, no
people live there permanently.

A RHYME ABOUT EUROPE

Its coastline is irregular,
with fjords
and bays and seas.
Europe's home
to Paris, Rome,
and cultured towns
like these.

A MATTER OF FACT

Europe is the sixth-largest continent.

Its biggest countries are Russia, Ukraine, and France.

One amazing feature: Europe is home to the world's smallest country, Vatican City. It is 0.17 square miles (0.44 sq. km) and is located inside Rome, Italy.

EXTRA CREDIT

Paris is the capital of France. Rome is the capital of Italy.

A RHYME ABOUT AUSTRALIA

It's hot in December.
They ski in July.
It has kangaroos, dingoes, and steers.
Aboriginal people
have called it their home
for thousands and thousands of years.

A MATTER OF FACT

Australia is the seventh-largest continent. That means it's the smallest continent.

Its biggest country is Australia. (Australia is the only country on the continent.)

One amazing feature: Aboriginal people have been living in Australia for more than thirty thousand years.

EXTRA CREDIT

For countries in the Southern Hemisphere (south of the equator), the seasons are the reverse of the seasons in the Northern Hemisphere (north of the equator). So Australia, South Africa, Brazil, and many other countries have summer in December and winter in July.

OH, CANADA!

Canada has ten provinces and three territories. The ten provinces in order from west to east are:

BRItish Columbia, **Alberta**, **SA**skatchewan, **MA**nitboa, **Ontario**, **QU**ebec, **NEW** Brunswick, **PRINCE** Edward Island, **NO**va Scotia, and **NE**wfoundland and Labrador.

BRIan
And SAm
MAde
Our QUiet
NEW PRINCE
NOd NErvousLy

The three territories are:
Yukon Territory,
NOrthwest Territory, and
NUnavut.

You're
NOt
NUtty!

EXTRA CREDIT

Provinces and territories are not the same.
Provinces have a bit more power
than territories. Only provinces can vote on
changes to the Canadian constitution.

MIXED-UP WORLD

Rearrange the letters in each cartoon caption to answer these geographical riddles. Find the answers on page 46.

This is the capital of the Netherlands.

Rest, Madam!

This mountain is the tallest mountain on land in the world. It's located in the Himalayas, near Nepal and Tibet. It is 29,035 feet (8,850 m) tall.

(Hint: The answer is two words.)

Overseen mutt

EXTRA CREDIT: Mauna Kea in Hawaii is taller than this mountain, but 19,684 feet (6,000 m) of it is underwater!

It's the capital of Australia.

EXTRA CREDIT: Australia's largest city is Sydney, but Sydney is not the capital.

Barn race

Located at the South Pole, this icy continent is the site of the coldest temperature ever recorded on the planet—colder than -125°F (-87°C).

An attic car

READ ON:

Can't get enough of the cold? Check out *Life on the Ice* by Susan E. Goodman for more about the South Pole and the North Pole.

The longest river in the world is in Egypt, on the continent of Africa.

(Hint: Rearrange the four letters on the arrow sign to name the river.)

EXTRA CREDIT:
This river is about
4,160 miles
(6,693 km) long.

LINE

This is the
largest country in
Central America.

(Hint: Mexico is part
of North America—not
Central America.)

Iguana car

READ ON:
Taste the flavors of this region
in *Cooking the Central American
Way* by Alison Behnke.

THE NAVIGATION STATION

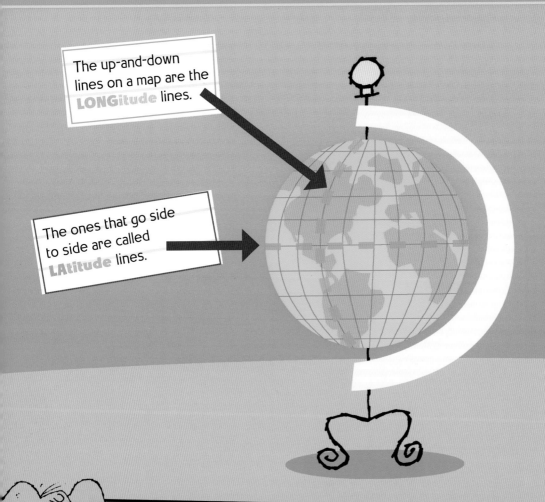

The up-and-down lines on a map are the **LONGitude** lines.

The ones that go side to side are called **LAtitude** lines.

EXTRA CREDIT

To find the latitude and longitude coordinates for your hometown, visit this site: http://geonames.usgs.gov/pls/gnispublic/. Type the name of the city in "Feature Name," select your state, and choose "Populated Place" in "Feature Class." Then click "Send Query"!

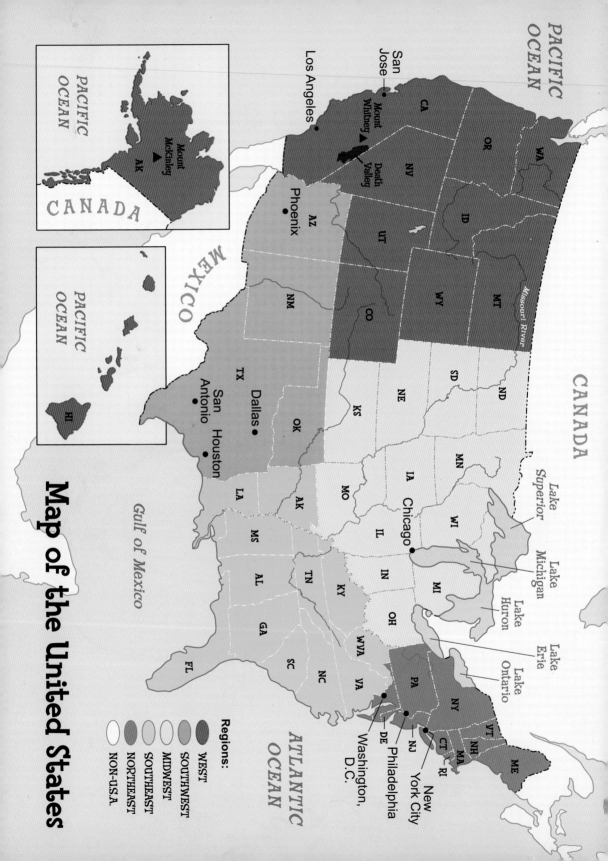

Map of the United States

Regions:
- WEST
- SOUTHWEST
- MIDWEST
- SOUTHEAST
- NORTHEAST
- NON-U.S.A.

PACIFIC OCEAN

PACIFIC OCEAN

PACIFIC OCEAN

CANADA

CANADA

MEXICO

ATLANTIC OCEAN

Gulf of Mexico

Mount McKinley ▲

AK

HI

Los Angeles
San Jose
San Francisco
Mount Whitney ▲
Death Valley
Phoenix

CA
NV
OR
WA
ID
UT
AZ
NM
CO
WY
MT
SD
ND
NE
KS
OK
TX
Dallas
San Antonio
Houston

Missouri River

Lake Superior
Lake Michigan
Lake Huron
Lake Erie
Lake Ontario

MN
IA
WI
MI
IL
IN
OH
MO
AK
LA
MS
AL
TN
KY
GA
SC
NC
FL
WVA
VA
PA
NY
VT
NH
MA
CT
RI
ME
DE
NJ

Chicago
Washington, D.C.
Philadelphia
New York City

Map of the World

Pacific Ocean

Arctic Ocean

RUSSIA

CHINA

Yangtze River

Mount Everest

INDIA

Caspian Sea

NETHERLANDS
UKRAINE

GREECE

Athens

Dead Sea

Mount Kilimanjaro

SUDAN

Nile River

ALGERIA

DEMOCRATIC REPUBLIC OF CONGO

Indian Ocean

AUSTRALIA

Sydney

Canberra

Southern Ocean

Amsterdam

Dublin

Paris

IRELAND

FRANCE

ITALY

Rome/Vatican City

Atlantic Ocean

Atlantic Ocean

NEWFOUNDLAND AND LABRADOR

NEW BRUNSWICK

PRINCE EDWARD ISLAND

Nova Scotia

QUEBEC

ONTARIO

MANITOBA

CANADA

ALBERTA

NORTHWEST TERRITORIES

YUKON TERRITORY

NUNAVUT

UNITED STATES

BRITISH COLUMBIA

SASKATCHEWAN

Mauna Kea (volcano in Hawaii)

UNITED STATES

MEXICO

Mexico City

NICARAGUA

VENEZUELA

Angel Falls

BRAZIL

PERU

ARGENTINA

Pacific Ocean

Continents:

ASIA

EUROPE

NORTH AMERICA

SOUTH AMERICA

AUSTRALIA

AFRICA

ANTARCTICA

OTHER

ANSWER KEY

MIXED-UP COUNTRY (pp. 20-23)

Yuck, lemon mint! = Mount McKinley

Tall, heavy Ed = Death Valley

Tiny women hut = Mount Whitney

Sir, our rim thieves! = the Missouri River

Weld area = Delaware

Rhino saddle = Rhode Island

Watchdogs Inn = Washington, D.C.

MIXED-UP WORLD (pp. 38-41)

Rest, Madam! = Amsterdam

Overseen mutt = Mount Everest

Hasten! = Athens

I spar. = Paris

Bun lid = Dublin

Barn race = Canberra

An attic car = Antarctica

Line = Nile

Iguana car = Nicaragua

GLOSSARY

archipelago: a group of islands (*see* p. 29)

bamboo: a plant that has a hard hollow stem and pointed leaves (*see* p. 29)

contiguous: things that are touching. The contiguous United States includes all the states except Alaska and Hawaii. (*see* p. 21)

continent: a large area of land. Earth's seven continents are Asia, Africa, North America, South America, Antarctica, Europe, and Australia. (*see* pp. 28-35, 41)

dingoes: wild dogs native to Australia (*see* p. 35)

equator: an imaginary line around the middle of Earth. The equator is halfway between the North Pole and the South Pole. (*see* pp. 30, 35)

fjords: narrow bodies of water connected to the ocean that are surrounded by steep cliffs. Norway, a country in Europe, is known for its fjords. (*see* p. 34)

latitude lines: horizontal lines on a map. These lines show how far north or south of the equator something is. (*see* pp. 42-43)

longitude lines: vertical lines on a map. These lines run from the North Pole to the South Pole. (*see* pp. 42-43)

navigation: using maps, compasses, and other tools to guide a ship, airplane, or other vehicle (*see* p. 42)

Northern Hemisphere: the part of Earth that is north of the equator (*see* p. 35)

plain: flat, grassy land (*see* p. 31)

plateau: a flat area of land that rises higher than the land around it (*see* p. 29)

provinces: similar to states. The United States of America is made up of fifty states, while Canada is made up of ten provinces and three territories. (*see* pp. 36-37, 45)

Southern Hemisphere: the part of Earth that is south of the equator (*see* p. 35)

steer: a young male of the domestic cattle family raised especially for its beef (*see* p. 35)

superior: better than something else (*see* pp. 4-5, 10)

territories: places that are controlled by a group or a government (*see* pp. 36-37, 45)

volume: how much space an object takes up (*see* p. 10)

READ ON!

BOOKS

Behnke, Alison. *Cooking the Central American Way.* Minneapolis: Lerner Publications Company, 2005.

Goodman, Susan E. *Life on the Ice.* Minneapolis: Millbrook Press, 2006.

Hamilton, Janice. *Canada.* Minneapolis: Lerner Publications Company, 2008.

Krensky, Stephen. *Anansi and the Box of Stories.* Minneapolis: Millbrook Press, 2007.

Streissguth, Tom. *Mexico.* Minneapolis: Lerner Publications Company, 2008.

Streissguth, Tom. *United States in Pictures.* Minneapolis: Twenty-First Century Books, 2008.

WEBSITES

CIA World Factbook
https://www.cia.gov/library/publications/the-world-factbook/index.html
Select a country to find a map and lots of key facts about the country.

Explore the States
http://www.americaslibrary.gov/cgi-bin/page.cgi/es
Choose a state and find out facts about that state and links to even more information.

Great Lakes Facts and Figures
http://www.great-lakes.net/lakes/ref/lakefact.html
Find plenty of facts and figures about the Great Lakes, as well as current conditions for each lake.

USA Geography—Map Game
http://www.sheppardsoftware.com/web_games.htm
This site offers games to test your knowledge of U.S. capitals, states, and landscapes.

Visual Geography Series
http://www.vgsbooks.com
If you're writing a report about a foreign country, be sure to visit this site. It offers downloads of photos, maps, and flags, report-writing tips, and links to much more information.

INDEX